# *Deciphering the Desert:*

## a book of poems

*by*

# Susan Cummins Miller

*Finishing Line Press*
Georgetown, Kentucky

# *Deciphering the Desert:*

## a book of poems

Publisher: Leah Huete de Maines
Editor: Christen Kincaid
Cover Art: Susan Cummins Miller
Author Photo: Susan Cummins Miller
Cover Design: Elizabeth Maines McCleavy


Order online: www.finishinglinepress.com
also available on amazon.com

Author inquiries and mail orders:
Finishing Line Press
P. O. Box 1626
Georgetown, Kentucky 40324
U. S. A.

# Table of Contents

*For my family members, friends and teachers, past and present,
who have shared their curiosity about the earth and its history,
along with their love of music and the written word*

# 1.

Above the portal
of my childhood library
timeless words chiseled
in stone beckon: "Be made whole
by great spaces and the stars."

# The Sculpture

In one corner
of the darkened stall
a narrow beam illumines black
serpentine rain-spirit—totemic miracle
of curving lines and edgy
synergy.

Incised tears slip
from onyx eyes transmuted
by meditation. Excoriation reveals
lumpen humanism, perfunctory, fleshy
immanence, ungainly
sensuality.

I hear a sibilant whisper. *Heed this,*
he says: *Whatever embarrasses*
*you is a subject ripe*
*for art.*

# Dreamtime

Late-night dream while singing along
to the last movement of Beethoven's *Ninth:*

An inch under the rim in mesa
moonshadow, in the presence
of lightning and Jupiter's rising,
the night awakens peregrine dreams:
a woman's-eye view, flying over
a sandpainting in Desolation Canyon.

The mandala of the great unknown
is a field guide to the rainbow
road, to the trail leading back
to Eve's journey from Eden, to desert
time, woven in stone: This is how
the world was given—

All treachery, treason, love, sacrifice,
tangos, searches, and loss
have been recorded in the bone manual,
in the lives of the cells, in the bittersweet,
separate intimacies of the survivor's
bible. Ahead lie

the valleys of dry bones and shining
stones. Ahead, scoured by the west
wind, lie a thousand leagues of blue water,
snow-capped mountains, canyons
of color and tainted hills. The choice
is mine.

Last exit to eagle beliefs and holy
places, to tough times along the killing
way, to split images and temporary
homelands, to a minimalist abode
or ancient ruins under scattered
clouds. No matter how

the world was given to us
down through the millennia,
the choice is mine.

# La Brea Woman: A Conversation

Partial skeleton, hidden
away—twenty-something woman
wearing dignity like a cloak despite
fractured skull, despite burial
in a hydrocarbon shroud for more than
nine thousand years—

questions rise like bubbles
in the tar pits, popping
when they meet air: What did you taste?
Where did you go? Whom
did you meet? What surprised you, brought
delight? What did your laugh sound like?

Did you have hopes? Did you
dream? Did you watch for a lover
who never returned? Did you have children?
Like me, did you make promises—
so many promises—you couldn't keep?

Did you make music? Did you wander
the silky, salty, grace notes
of sound? Did you ponder
the cool earth of possibilities? Did you wonder,
ancient woman who lived on the fringe
and returned to the light in a megalopolis?

Were you curious? Did you ask questions?
Did you feel the subtle shift in tenor
when answers appeared, as if
from the very air? Did you feel
the ground shake and flow
underfoot? Did you feel terror?

The air today is pregnant
with answers, the equifinality
of end-time mind-melding: *Yes, yes, yes,*

the wind whispers in the fluttering
gum trees. *Yes, yes,*
*Yes.*

# Once upon a Time in the West


Black-and-white Buick station wagon pulling
a matching Aljo trailer from California
to Minnesota in 1953. Parents up front, three kids
on the middle seat, the two youngest, myself included,

in the roomy back end. We started each leg of the journey
with a prayer to the phosphorescent plastic Jesus
Mom stuck on the dashboard, then counted off (in Spanish),
just to make sure no one was left behind. Once, distracted,

we forgot to pray and count till we were ten miles
down the road. We reversed course to recover
my tiny sister who stood, bawling,
on the gas station curb. She's never forgiven

her siblings for failing to notice she wasn't there.
But when, years later, we sort through
our parents' effects, which one of us tearfully claims
that glow-in-the-dark plastic Jesus?

## Buttons and Shells

Mother,
when Logan's school shirt needed tending
last night I opened the sewing box—
you remember, that Robert Burns
Black-Watch cigar-box full
of multicolored plastic and pearl
buttons you bought, forty years ago,
for shirtwaists and wool skirts.

In one corner I found
three seashells, cowries
from the winter beach
at Carpinteria—shells no bigger
than my thumbnail, shells of cream
and palest brown too small to whisper
sea sounds in my ear, shells
that were the prizes when we strolled
hard sand in silence
hand in hand.

# The Badger

My boots sink deep
in gray-green shale cloaked
with a stubble of Idaho hay, rousing
a badger who, shoulders braced
and claws splayed, straddles
the narrow cow-path, hisses
through sharp-cusped teeth, contending
for this patch of earth as fiercely
as my sister claimed the bottom bunk
while I gave ground, unwilling
to fight, unwilling to lose
another chunk of flesh.

Today I stand
my ground. The badger lunges,
snorts, before retreating
to her den.

# When Jeanette MacDonald Reigned in the Kitchen


A winter evening in '62.
My sister, sixteen—the trailing edge

of innocence—dawdles
over dishwashing, knit sleeves pushed up, lifts

a handful of bubbles from the sink
and sends them soaring

on drifts of song: *"O sweet mystery*
*of life at last I've found you."*

# To My Parents, with Gratitude

You made me
a child of the woods
and deserts, offered antidotes
to cleithrophobia and claustrophobia,
to the limits of stone blocks and brick, plastered
wood and asphalt, to formulaic
schoolroom texts.

You taught me to focus
on breathing, on light and distance.
You taught me to embrace space, to narrow vision
to a pinpoint aperture. From innumerable
starry nights and dusty trails, riverside
camps and granite tarns, from strikes
of trout and kokanee on hooks
and lures, from the smell of Baja grunion,
floured and seasoned, frying

in a cast-iron skillet, I absorbed
the rattlesnake truth, inspired
and inspiring, yet always requiring
groundwork: *Access it, identify it, name it,*
*shout it*—

all sounds lost in the vastness
of Pacific swells, isolated beaches, gorges
deeper and larger than San Francisco
canyons, sound lost in mud-choked
virgin rivers, among arches and badlands,
red cliffs and yellow stone, grand
canyons and glaciers—sound muffled
by redwoods, sequoias, digger pines, cedars,
and Joshua trees.

Even now, so many years
later, a photograph, a snatch
of song, a snippet of poetry, a map

or a place name triggers
joy like the sustained warmth
of an embrace, like a tug
on the other end of time.

# 2.

## Reflections

Monsoon clouds deliver male rain,
coaxing life from parched soil. Brown puddles,
spawning grounds for spadefoot toads
(hoarsely seeking, loudly mating),
mirror double rainbows in denim sky.

# Wilderness Bloomed There

Wilderness bloomed there
in the curve of the driveway
in the shadow of a post
hidden from dog-walkers and commuters
and the curtained windows
of cinder-block homes: a pincushion
cactus, *Mammillaria*, wearing a crown
of purple blossoms. The nondescript plant
has been hiding in plain sight, small
and all but forgotten

like a student from a foreign land
who sits silently, all semester, at the back
of the lecture hall, the force within her building
until, one day, she raises her hand
speaks aloud
and the world turns to stare
in surprise
in awe.

# The Bone-Man's Apprentice

Between Route 66
and the Old Spanish Trail
we hiked serrated ridges, discovering
a cache of fossil bones preserved
on a limy sandstone ledge
in the heart of the Mojave.

Under your watchful eye
I chiseled away the barren, protective strata,
exposing teeth and dimpled bone—a horse's skull
no longer than my hand, concealed
for eighteen million years. With clear drops
of Glyptol, I sealed the fragile fragments.

You showed me how to swaddle the delicate palate
in layers of TP, how to mix the Plaster of Paris.
I poured tepid canteen water into the dented basin, added
pale-gray powder that smelled like kindergarten, warmed
numb fingers in the exothermic reaction, dipped strips
of rough brown burlap in the thick white soup.

Laughing, we smoothed the gooey paste
on fossil and rock pedestal, our fingers
and forearms taking on the virginal hue until
neither of us could identify
where our bodies ended
and the sun-bleached hills began.

# Once upon an Idaho Mountaintop

Midsummer fieldwork: Schmid Ridge—
as western as the red dust seeping through
the seams and cracks of a well-used Jeep,
coating the fine hairs of my forearms.
A wide-mouthed moon rises late.

Fog fills the well
of the Blackfoot River valley. Early sunlight sparkles
like zircon on dew-drenched grass and scrub running halfway
up the slope. No breeze. Thrust-faulted limestone, chert,
and sandstone wall above: a forty-minute climb

just to reach the point
I left off mapping yesterday. Stumping and sweating
my way up this new trail, measuring
the strike and dip of strata as I go. At the top, along the edge
of the ridge, sheep graze, tugging up grass, roots and all.

A doe startles from her bed
among the aspen. One could read meaning into that island
of Rex Chert in the middle of a pasture far below, glimpsed
as the fog burns away. Or into that stretch
of dirt road, leading to a junction.

At just such a fork, viewed from a bus window
on the way to Delphi's limestone hills,
Oedipus met a stranger—triggering
an odyssey and setting in motion
all that was to happen later.

## Two Roads Diverged

Dodging raindrops and lightning bolts
I ducked into the split-log bar
in Montello. Bud Country, but Dave
rustled up a warm Guinness
from the back.

My brown hair was long then, twisted
up off my neck and secured
with a piece of leather
and a wooden pick, sharpened
at both ends.

Played pool with three geologists
and a cowboy—just a way to pass the time,
a way to drive the geologic puzzles
from my mind so I could sleep. Lost,
on both counts.

Walking back to the motel
in the sultry darkness, under restless stars,
the Leach Mountains at my back
the valley stretching east forever—
or to Utah,

whichever came first—I passed
that cowboy, smoking behind the store.
He tossed out a proposition
like a half-smoked Camel.
Unfiltered.

The wind riffled the cottonwood leaves.
Black shadows played tag. A killdeer piped
from the sage-covered slope.
A horned owl answered.
Awkwardly,

laughing, I turned on my heel,
grinding the metaphorical butt
into the muddy road. Yet,
thirty years later, I'm still
wondering.

# Mapping Murdoch Mountain, Nevada

Crossing the Permo-Triassic boundary,
an angular unconformity, the earth's version
of a clean slate: a few feet of rock strata
capture the uncertainty of animation

where only ten per cent of species survive.
On one side of the hiatus—millions of years
of missing time—the last evidence of the slow evolution
of creatures that once ruled the seas. Nearly all

of the lineages of trilobites, ammonites and brachiopods
vanish—swept away, as though by Merlin's
wand. Across the boundary, the future: new bivalves,
gastropods and vertebrates explore and colonize

vacant niches—digging, swimming, planting wild
new habitats, showing the pliant toughness
of intrepid life. Nature abhors a vacuum, seeking instead:
balance, and the mercy of the unknown.

# Genesis

Remember when we climbed that limestone tor
out in Nevada? Craving privacy
and summer-hardened bodies we spread your
chambray work shirt under aging pine trees
to shield our naked skin from needles, twigs
and time-etched talus. Afterwards, your head
soft-pillowed on my thigh, we shared ripe figs,
red apples, water—canteen-warm—and bread.
We stared at skies where falcons flew. You tried
to speak—a croak. I brushed ants from my boot.
"This doesn't mean I'll marry you," you cried,
then shied from me and bit into the fruit.
The silence grew about us, hot and still.
We lobbed half-eaten apples down the hill.

# Unharvested Water

Gila Wilderness, 6 p.m.
Thunder's an oak barrel rolling
down cliffs, drawing me into
the storm. Buffeting wind. Mist
on bare skin. Quicksilver cloud-surge
on ancient caldera.

Raindrops thrum differently
on tin roofs, trailer shells
and faded canvas tents.
This Tuesday evening
drops sizzle like burgers
on that roadside grill
in Oasis, Nevada.
Maybe if I hadn't stopped there
on the way back from town
I'd have caught you
before you struck camp. Maybe.
But would it have changed things?

Unharvested water
courses down trails, ponds
in the low places, seeps
between sand grains
displacing stale air,
collecting like old regrets,
in the starless, secret places
where no one
can pitch a tent.

# Memorial Day for a Compromised Planet

i.

The sun rises orange,
screened by smoke from the fires
enveloping the western states.
Somewhere in the world

poets are dying
because they speak fire: Words
that lay bare the truth
of what is and what is not.

ii.

Toads await the thrumming
of the rain on crusty earth.

*This is my time,* the circling
vulture signs. The fear is this:

Soon the desert denizens
will have no memory of water.

iii.

The Eighth Plague strikes at noon
when a flatbed truck overturns
on I-10. Twenty million bees escape,

eclipsing sun, turning day
to twilight, hovering, confused—finding
freedom as potent as honey mead.

iv.

The scarlet wings of a Pepsis wasp trace
a crazy path of figure-8s and water signs, winding down,
going no place. Did her sleek black body lay one egg

on some tarantula's thorax to nurture larvae
through the winter? Or will she die barren, genes
removed from a dwindling pool?

Life is such a fragile affair, survival and success
subject to Nature's whims. We cycle through
like a bougainvillea blossom drifting

on turbulent air, that comes to rest between
two lizards sunning on a riprap wall
before sliding out of sight.


v.

At the end of the day, hope rises
in the form of an Anna's hummingbird, black
against the dimming sky, who halts

her beating wings atop the highest branch
of a mesquite: a miracle of alert,
shining stillness.

# Writing among the Ruins

i. Betatakin Cliff Dwellings

Kaolinite. Montmorillonite. Illite. Common clays
that, when mixed with water and temper, serve
to raise pottery walls enclosing nothing.
Earth holding air.

But once, this simple vessel cradled
and transported maize kernels, beans, bones, or water—
the triumph of creativity over the struggle to endure,
to feed, to leave offspring.

No signature identifies the artisan
of this simple, undecorated olla—only
a thumbprint, surviving the pit fire,
surviving time.


ii. Chaco Canyon

Bones lie under curtains
of sandstone—makeshift sarcophagi—light denied
the nameless essences, fleshly contents dissipated,
disintegrated. On this day, no one

leaves flowers or chants prayers for naked shades
in this place where trails converge—pathways
engineered as straight as the walls that once marked
the passing of the solstice flare.

A rare autumn raindrop, anointing oil
for fragile bones, finds access between thin-
bedded blocks. Do the stones remember
echoed conversations—songs, the laughter

of children, the wails of mourning women?
The capricious wind keens with whispers, sharing
long-lost intrigues, sharing the reasons
the ancients abandoned their dead.

# 3.

Wind blows empty nest
from palm frond. Doves collect twigs
for reconstruction.

## Up Lightning Creek

My mother's hands,
age-spotted yet supple
as willow withes,
pluck huckleberries
in dense thickets.

Hiking boots find purchase
on the clear-cut slope. Tooled leather belt
clasps an improvised bucket:
recycled Folgers can.
Bailing-wire handle.

Interspersing family tales
with jam and cobbler recipes, she strips
the bushes clean, her laughter
rich, robust enough to scare
the bears away. Forever.

Bucket filled,
her blue-stained fingers split
a ham-on-rye, offering communion
and one final
benediction.

# Angle of Reflection

At Priest Lake
early summer energies fuse
at the water line: keel meets
reflected keel; mountain slips
into inverted mountain; dipping strata
and angled rock conjoin.

Tell me
which is reality—rock?
Reflection? I touch
rock's hardness, taste its clay, yet see
each mirrored contact, crystal
repeated in exact detail.

So tell me
when I photograph reflections
do I seek to capture
that elusive boundary between what is
and what will be? Between what is
and what can be?

Tell me—does *passing over*
simply mean crossing the line
that separates
one dimension from another?
The world has gone crazy.
I need to know.

The boat at the dock
sinks low in the water
sliding beneath that vital line
just as my father, energy fading
seems halfway to
another plane.

# The Waiting Game

In the season of dream
I'm waiting
like a threadbare cabin
with nobody home
standing in a canyon furrowed
by rillwash, dwarfed
by brutal sky.

In the season of nightmare
I'm waiting
binding wounds with hardscrabble hope
handknit scarves and silver duct tape
while raindrops crash
noisy as fists
on a flat tin roof—waiting
for one arrow of sunlight
to steal between the shafts
of rain.

*Breathe*
sighs a gust of wind
redolent with creosote
and desert willow.
*If you just breathe*
*wonder will follow.*

# One Night and a Quarter of Tomorrow

The night you left us
the smoke trees wore a cloud
of tiny lavender blossoms
that looked gray and insubstantial
in the moonlight.

After the late-night news,
you and I sat on the porch, watching
the creamy saguaro buds unfold
as slowly as a solemn high Mass.
You told me how it pained you
that those flowers
had this one night
and a quarter of tomorrow
before they closed for good.
A microcosm
of a woman's life.

That's all I remember
except that it was Mother's Day
and I'd brought no gift—
just myself, sitting next to you
on the porch swing, listening
to the old stories one last time—
how you skinny-dipped
with your sisters in warm
Minnesota lakes, sang
with a big band at college, fished
for pike with Boppa . . .

We rocked and laughed together
until, around midnight,
the bats fluttered in
to bury their wrinkled faces
in the soft saguaro blossoms
overflowing with pollen.

# There Will Never Be Enough

There will never be enough words
for light. But I know

what this is not, this luminous light evolving
in the gradual dawning

of a springtime Sonoran desert day. This light
hasn't the harshness

of midsummer noontime—shadowless
and sere, impaling sahuaros ripe

with purple fruit—nor the warm glow
of miniature Christmas lights wrapped

around the branches of a Noble Fir. This is not
the pale, insipid beam emitted

by a flashlight, and it's brighter than the flames
of votive candles flickering in slanted racks

before the Virgin of Guadalupe. This light has
the presence and texture of rays

that streamed through clerestory windows
into my childhood church, throwing

varicolored stains on marble aisles, sculptures, altars.
This light, this dawnlight, transports

the full, deep, nacreous numinosity
of the rosary beads I tucked into

the chest pocket of my mother's hospital gown
as I watched her final breath lift off.

# Pass It on

Our lives are about what it takes
to navigate this world: Good sense
of direction. Modest place
in the layered hills. A glimpse
of the blind dizziness of evolving

life forms in lost environments captured
in rocks beside a thousand trails.
The red road meanders
through time and space. Tell
your children stories about the time before time.

Take them on a ramble into the mountains.
Breathe deep the rich air. Lift binoculars, sharpen
the focus, close the distance, explain the faults
and fossils. Pass it on: Through those lessons
enter the sea once more, backstroke

to life's horizon on the tremulous sand.
Recount how, in the eons since, tectonic plates
opposed, separated, collided—grinding
against resistance in an endless cycle
of reformation.

They are the world. Pass it on.
One sentient life is just long enough
to begin the journey toward understanding
what we've been given
and what we've lost.

## The Asperger's Art of Blending in

In the laundry room I fold
my son's clean tee-shirts, Amish-plain
solids in muted colors.

On the patio a gecko
races over sandstone that's wrinkled
and pink as a newborn's skin. He leaves

no footprint, makes no sound. Camouflaged
he slides between the border rocks, merges
with verbena shadow and damp brown earth.

How clever, how safe
to live unseen: an earth-toned creature
in a dusky land.

## Reality Bites

We stood
that Tuesday morning
like twin towers, shoulders touching,
watching as the second plane hit. Then
you grabbed your lunch bag
and ran for the bus.

All day long
I sat, without rocking,
in the rocking chair.
I couldn't write. I lost
my taste for food.

"I feel like
I've been raped," you said,
when you came home
from school. Old eyes now gazed
from your boy-man's face.

Never
had you let me hug you so hard
or for so long.

*for Logan*

## Note to an Autistic Son

A drop of ink—black
as deepest thought, black as fear
in the lee side of midnight
and the ash-choked runoff
from scorched mountainsides—
a drop of ink clings
to the tip of my pearl-gray pen
poised above innocent paper.

What can I say
to convince you to cast
your emotional chain mail aside?
What can I write
to persuade you to trust—to risk
and risk again? It hurts,
I know. But the world is awash
in ink, my son, so tell me
your story. Please.

Let words fall, harsh
and bitter, tangy as soy sauce,
sweetly smooth as mole. There's an ocean
of ink in this world, son—enough red
for the depths of pain, enough blue
for ten thousand rejections.
Let words fall from a heart
that has held them too long.
Let loose your story.
I'll wait.

# Veterans Day, Tucson

At the intersection
of River and Swan, a woman sits
on the concrete island, holding a sign
penned on a piece of cardboard box:

> *Stranded. 2 hungry children*
> *to feed. Please help.*

A man in faded olive drab sits, cross-legged
next to her. He chugs from a bottle swathed
in a plastic grocery bag, lights her cigarette
from his own, holds up a matching cardboard flap:

> *Vietnam Vet. Unrecovering alcoholic.*
> *$1 = Bud + bagel. God Bless America.*

A motorcycle officer eases into
the left-turn lane, hands them something—
a dollar? a ticket? an address for a shelter?—
and asks them to move on.

Their laughter dissipates like smoke
in the mild November air. "Thank you,"
the man says and collects
his scant belongings.

At home I shred tortillas, toss them
to doves and quail who cry, *Why? Why?*
as if for David and Patrick and all the names
inscribed on a wall in Washington—boys

no older than my sons, boys
who didn't return, if only to sit,
cross-legged, holding a sign
at River and Swan.

# 4.

## *Deep Purple*

Late night.
Phantom cries
      from empty rooms.
Cold moon
      on leafless mesquite.
Snatches of melody
      through half-closed windows.
It was your song.

# News

What's different
about this morning?

A verdin's feather clings
to velvet mesquite thorn,
bean pods rain upon the deck
and rustle as they bounce
and settle. A pair of gilded flickers
squawks in the palm crown, noisy
in their breakfasting.
The orchid blooms all faded
overnight.

A black-chinned hummingbird
has taken residence
among the pale-pink oleander
and crimson bottle brush;
sulfur-yellow butterflies
play tag above lantana beds, mating
on the wing; and yesterday,
you tell me,
Molcie died.

Underneath
my window
one scented white gardenia
opens.

# The Packrat's Nest

Outside, rain falls
on the packrat's nest under
my window. Winter has stripped
the leaf umbrella, exposing
human and plant debris—
a model recycling project of twigs, bark
and soggy gym socks, snug and warm
and smelly as that old canvas tent we shared
on the limestone bluffs
of Nevada.

I'm convinced
that at this moment, somewhere
under the Great Basin stars, packrats gather
lost dreams. If only we could journey back
to Willow Creek, perhaps we'd find,
amidst the sage, the point
our paths diverged.

# After You Left

Listening
to Lara Nyro and Nina Simone:
bared blue-soul musings, tones
like raw silk brushed with tears.

Hungry notes glitter
with empty-room bravado before pulling back
beneath whispered skin. Lyrics reveal
what loneliness engenders

in bruised hearts and tortured psyches—reveal
lonely rivers of pain, meandering aimlessly,
reveal understanding, just beyond reach,
just beyond good-bye.

# On the Divide

How many times have I crossed
the Continental Divide? Two hundred? Three?

The Highway to the Sun at Waterton-Glacier.
Lolo Pass in the Bitterroots. Butte City, Yellowstone,
and ghostly South Pass City where the wind whistled
through sage and prairie bluestem, violent stories echoed
in narrow alleyways between weather-beaten
buildings, and somewhere a shutter banged
like the crack of a gunshot.

I remember a steep climb up and over
Wolf Creek Pass in the San Juans. And later,
driving the flatlands flanking the highway
west of Deming, New Mexico, a road sign
the only evidence I'd traversed the subtle rise
separating rivers flowing east from rivers
flowing west. Duality made manifest.
There is no east without west, no joy
without sorrow, no life without death, no
action without reaction.

Here, on the Divide near Silver City, I park
on the crest of a switchback road. The wind soughs
softly through sapless pines. Dead trees talking.
The closed mine's silent trucks guard
a wasteland of disemboweled
earth. The raw wound gapes, exposed
as an open grave awaiting
the casket.

# Cracking the Code

i.

Starting out, hard pavement consumes
wishes and hopes—polarizes, compresses
emotion: Too little time to make space

for us. Too little time
to make changes. The burning
tragedy of too little time.

ii.

Itinerant workers prune
our old willow, revealing boles bending

in opposite directions: north toward
the mountains, south toward the light.

iii.

The gardener pontificates,
arms waving. One plant thrives. Another
dies. It's all about

roots: shoving between pebbles, cobbles,
boulders and sand, poking, prying, reaching, gripping,
sucking moisture, thrusting caliche aside, leaching

precious nutrients from clay and rock. Interstices
yield wiggle room—tiny hairs, sensitive
as mole whiskers, send coded messages to probing

root tip and anchor elegant saguaro standing, arms uplifted
to sun and stars, to air and rain, tomorrow
and today—unflinching. It's about roots.

iv.

I lock the door on the double-dreaming
past, on flashy simplicity, aloof
contemporary fare, temporary decor damnably
full of faux everything—

a single row of pictures and understated
wallpaper in a sky-lit room, subliminally
pandering to the adolescent sexuality
in time-worn allegories. Locking the door's

a grassroots movement that leaves
no trace. Action creates obvious uneasiness,
but who doesn't love the raw power, the erotic
asymmetry of starting over?

## Communion

No path but the journey. No
destination but the desert garden
beyond knowing. There, I will meet

you. There, we will walk and talk and eat
hummus, tikka masala, and shepherd's pie.
There, we will drink cool water

and hot tea spiced with mint
grown in pots around a pool. There,
our words will find common ground.

# Limbo

Under the whimpering skies of June earth lolls
and licks parched lips. In the shadow
of Baboquivari, where I'itoi dwells
in his cave, the Tohono O'odham harvest
saguaro fruit with elongated wooden crosses
while my children cry
for respite from the heat.

When will monsoon rains
end dry endless spring?

The wind slides restlessly
between the stunted cornstalks. A pale moon
yawns. Behind the granite mountain front
where black hawks dive and bears raid
Igloo coolers, male clouds lurk—building,
toning, bunching, flexing, thrusting,
breeding hail.

St. John's Day passes. The air-tide
turns. At dusk arroyos drown, white lightning
lances peaks, old women sing,
my brown feet dance.

## Breaking the Legacy

Once, here, a legacy of silence and disbelief
reigned in a barren sanctuary, held in thrall
to rolling clouds shunted aside
by strong emotions, to bitter memories
beyond pale waters, to darkness hemmed
by milky light. But not tonight,

when moon-thread entangles,
interlaces raised arms, breaks out
on the river of a poem—clamoring
like a heart bursting with echoes
summoned from sea-swept boulders
where waves shimmer with phosphorescence.

Uncertain waters rise in vapor swirls
of gauze fog, spiral upward in a dance as old
as deep time. Solemn Nature, paper-light body,
shells cupped to both ears, opens her mouth
to sing an anthem in praise of truth:
Among wildfires, hurricanes, tornados,

drought, floods, pandemics, rising sea levels
and temperatures, species decimation and retreating
glaciers, there is only now—
now to rally believers and skeptics
behind outspoken scientists, now
to hold the line.

# There Is More Here

Fierce winds sculpt nearby dunes, erasing
all tracks. Hot golden sunlight burns off
thick mists and the sweet dew
of early morning. Shadows race
over crashing Pacific swells
where fresh and salt waters collide:

If we could back-trace this rivulet
to its source—through legend, art, and ancient
hints etched and pecked into bone relics, desert
varnish and smoke-caked limestone walls—
what mysteries would we witness? What origin-
songs would tremble on air currents?

What would we know without being taught?
There is more here. Always.
See how one smooth pebble lies prone
on raw, unforgiving basalt cliffs—as out of place
and inexplicable as fleshy fears extending,
stretching this pleated soul.

# The Writer Retreats

Only in silence
can I regain the precious sense
of words, the weighty value
of each syllable, the sacredness
of spoken thought.

Only in stillness
will I hear the *chuk'-kah*
of anxious quail, the arrogant whistle
of curve-billed thrasher, the sigh
of breezes currying dust
from new-laid granite gravel,
the scratch of a desert whiptail's toes
on rhyolite cobbles that border
the path outside
my hermitage.

Only in stillness
will I hear the saguaro
drawing in upon itself
as first light stains the waiting sky
above the Rincon Mountains.

Only in silence, only in stillness
can I hear my heart's percussion—the paradiddle
urging me down the path
that appears now
between the cholla
and the prickly pear.

# 5.

Azure butterfly,
safe on petals of blue-eyed
grass, unfolds new wings.

# Entering the Mojave

Where ancient seas
once split a continent, asphalt highways link
a far-flung people. With shuttered eyes
the hordes pass through.

This ruptured crust,
this dry land, drowning in its own debris,
is far too hot, too cold, inhospitable,
too barren, thorny, inconsiderate.

Here, we cannot hide
in the shadows of tall oaks and poplars,
our voices are not muffled by the rush of water
over stones.

We who stop
must face our scars
from wounds incised like petroglyphs
on wrinkled skin of upthrust rock.

Or turn away,
to lose ourselves in cities
where neon lights obscure and shadows reveal
half-truths and obsequies.

And yet, this land
of hoodoos and phantom lakes bewitches,
promising a solitude
more precious than rain.

So I escape
into empty canyons, climb
the desert-varnished ledges, bare my head
to unsheltering sky.

I draw deep
the untainted air, let the unrelenting sun
suck poison from my soul,
let pain melt

into mirage,
set my dreams adrift
on thermals, watch them rise
to mingle with the stars.

# Aubade

I read the morning
as I would a book, scent
by scent, leaf by leaf, sound
and color and changing light
transfixing
me as I descend, drawing
images after me
until I glow
like a tin-framed mirror
in an old adobe rancho.

# Pandemic Echoes

Life hides
under the audible thumps, quavers,
songs & sobs of everyday
cacophony. Escape lies in the solitary—
in the ordinary pace of footsteps starting
a journey along imaginary ley lines
to forever islands of contemplation:

a trail of clouds—
gray-bottomed, wispy, sharp-edged—
leads from sunrise to sunset, pointing
like an arrow shaft, as if the sun
might lose its way.

Possibility enters
the world in silences—thought
swelling with ink into life, into words
mouthed without sound, hummed
at a pitch so lofty it resonates
with the amaranthine music
of the spheres.

# In the Land of Little Rain

With throaty calls
two cactus wrens construct a nest
twig by pilfered twig
on staghorn cholla. A house finch sings

atop mesquite. The warm breeze scatters
hard palm seeds on path and patio,
dirt and grass, like beads
from a broken rosary.

Dust coats the coral aloe buds
and barrel cactus fruit; the dry air desiccates
the prickly pear. But, as if to spite the drought
a single drop of dew

clings to a strand of spider silk stretched
between agave leaves. The tiny prism carries hope
in every color, every hue, and draws the eye
beyond to where, high

in the burning western sky, Venus glides
in graceful transit
across the glowing surface
of the sun.

# A Day of Questions without Answers: Sonoran Desert

i.

From saguaro crown
two Gila woodpeckers call:
Same notes. Disparate
keys. What secrets—what sublime
mysteries—lie hidden
in those differences?

ii.

My coral top confuses
one stray hummingbird
who ventures close, expecting
subtle scents of aloe flower. Life
is like that, isn't it: Expectations
rarely meeting outcome? But when
the two collide, how sweet
the nectar tastes.

iii.

Hurrying west on St. Mary Street
in rush-hour traffic, Venus and Jupiter
glowing low over Tumamoc Hill,
when suddenly a shooting star, a vagrant
from the farthest reaches
of the solar system, keeps pace
for ten seconds before flaring out.

What secrets could it tell
of time before time? Or, was it just
an astronaut's tool kit
coming home?

iv.

All day strong winds bent palm fronds
into giant Venus flytraps that spat
black seeds upon the deck. Now
even the birds are silent: The clamor
of spring and summer slid to a whisper
in autumn, then fell away completely
with the sycamore leaves.

Do you suppose, in this pre-winter hush,
that somewhere birdsongs collect in drifts
against a weathered snow fence—
caught fast till spring unlatches
an invisible gate and winds rearrange
the jumbled notes into old arias
pitched at a level only birds can hear?

# Into Saguaro National Park-West

i.

Cloud waves, rosy-tinted
in first dawnlight, break upon
the atmospheric western shore.
A great horned owl calls
from the ancient saguaro, spreads its wings
and glides away to merge
with retreating shadows, while three tufts
of buffel grass wave outside
my hermitage window.

ii.

Entering the park via Picture Rocks Wash:
High above, the leading edges of clouds
curl like salt plumes. A male cardinal flutters
from branch to branch in a palo verde, bright scarlet
in the noonlight. He carries his secrets
to a small mesquite, pauses, head cocked, listening,
then glides behind a dacite bluff
as if returning home.

iii.

Late afternoon sunlight strikes
eternal figures etched
in desert varnish. Arms linked, they dance
around the Spiral, shuffling
to silent chants that set the still air thrumming,
while below their feet
the white sand river laps
frozen lava—flowing,
and not flowing.

# For Diana: On the Second Anniversary of Her Death

I rescued a gilded flicker
from your room of stone
and glass. Confused from crashing
into windowpanes she huddled
in a corner, beak pointing south.

You found a soft towel embroidered
with a smiling sun. Crawling under
the cherry-wood desk I wrapped
the flicker in a white cocoon, crooning
*Hush, hush, now, I won't hurt you—*

the same words I murmured
to my sons as I plucked cactus needles
from tiny fingers. The flicker quieted
in my scarred, weathered hands. As
you waited, barely breathing,

I carried her to the parapet, opened
the swaddling cloth and set her free.

# Seeking

Farewell:
To the downward motion
of rejecting thumb, the shouting,
the screech of traffic, the haze obscuring
blue skies and planets. I'm off
to devour the ordinary corners
of life (as long as none of them
are constructed with right angles).

Seeking:
To drown in a passion
for quiet places, to catch
a sudden meteor shower
from a memorial bench placed
on a short stretch of gravel road
where pencil-thin shadows tickle
the grin of a crescent moon
perched on a branch—

while, nearby, a vole scurries
across the new-mown field, finding shelter
under a pile of hay.

## Spider Woman

The spider spins
a single strand of red that floats
on desert winds whistling
through the succulents.

She does not think:
*How difficult it is to weave
a web on windy days.*

She simply climbs
that yucca leaf, lets go,
and trusts the anchor,
trusts the wind.

# Deciphering the Desert

Wandering, one foot before
the other, wind at my back
I find myself where I began.
The Rosetta stones

lay hidden in plain sight:
that sulphur-yellow butterfly
scouring an autumn flower bed
for one last sip of nectar;

a host of desert broom seeds
drifting overhead
like a soft November
blizzard; the story revealed

by a rust-stained sandstone
that went to bed in the sea
three hundred million years ago
and awoke in my garden.

# The Entropy of Water

Perambulating
on the whispering, saltating sand
between wave and stabilized dune, negotiating

dipping strata, weedy estuary, an overgrown trail.
Grateful to be haunted
by the waxing moon as I settle

on a Monterey cypress branch spanning
a tributary, knees wrapped around
water-worn knobs, exhausted legs quivering

like aspen leaves. Sharing the pause
with two robins squabbling over a worm.
Transfixed by seeds, mosses, twigs and leaves

drifting by: I can't explain why
I feel rooted to this earth-joining-sky
place, to the entropy of water

in babbling rivulets that leak, downstream,
into lagoon and sea. Searching
for forgiveness for not doing enough.

Finding a forgotten hunger for the vanished time
when we granted clemency to things
without speech. It is a hunger to remember,

to believe a time will come again
when we can drink from streams and rivers,
as we used to, or jump off trestle bridges, twirling

in air before plunging into pristine lakes,
as we used to—a time when we can laugh as we play
dimly remembered dare-games.

# Acknowledgments

I am grateful to the editors of the following publications in which the listed poems originally appeared, some in slightly different form:

*The Blue Guitar Magazine:* "La Brea Woman: A Conversation," "Mapping Murdoch Mountain, Nevada," "There Is More Here" and "Writing among the Ruins"

*Cathexis Northwest Press:* "After You Left" and "Into Saguaro National Park-West"

*Global Warming: Collection of Poems (Poets Choice):* "Memorial Day for a Compromised Planet" and "Breaking the Legacy"

*Impermanent Earth:* "The Entropy of Water"

*Iris Literary Journal:* "Dreamtime"

*New Texas 2009:* "News"

*More Voices of New Mexico* anthology (Rio Grande Books): "Unharvested Water"

*OASIS Journal:* "The Sculpture," "Buttons and Shells," "The Badger," "Wilderness Bloomed There," "Genesis," "Up Lightning Creek," "One Night and a Quarter of Tomorrow," "The Asperger's Art of Blending in," "Reality Bites," "Veterans Day, Tucson," "Aubade" and "Spider Woman"

Pima County Public Library: "Above the portal" and "Wind Blows Empty Nest"

*Roundup! Western Writers of America Presents Great Stories of the West from Today's Leading Western Writers* anthology (La Frontera Publishing): "Two Roads Diverged"

*Sandcutters:* "The Waiting Game"

*Sandcutters 2012 Contest Winners' Anthology* (Arizona State Poetry Society): "Note to an Autistic Son," "The Packrat's Nest" and "Entering the Mojave"

*SandScript 2009 Art and Literary Magazine:* "Angle of Reflection"

*Snapdragon:* "There Will Never Be Enough"

*Unstrung:* "To My Parents, with Gratitude," " On the Divide," "Limbo" and "For Diana: On the Second Anniversary of Her Death"

*What Wildness Is This: Women Write about the Southwest* anthology (The University of Texas Press): "The Bone-Man's Apprentice"

*The Write Launch:* "When Jeanette MacDonald Reigned in the Kitchen" and "Cracking the Code"

Tucson writer **Susan Cummins Miller** holds degrees in geology, history, and anthropology, with a focus on vertebrate paleontology and stratigraphy. She worked as a field geologist and taught geology and oceanography before turning to writing fiction, nonfiction, and poetry. She has been writer-in-residence at the Djerassi Resident Artists Program, Woodside, CA, and the Pima County Public Library, Tucson, AZ.

Miller is the author of the novels *Death Assemblage, Detachment Fault, Quarry, Hoodoo, Fracture* and *Chasm*, four of which were finalists for the WILLA Award in contemporary fiction. She compiled and edited *A Sweet, Separate Intimacy: women writers of the American frontier, 1800-1922*, a finalist for the Longan Award, and received the Tucson Poetry Festival's Will Inman Award. Her poetry, essays, and short fiction have appeared in, or are forthcoming in, numerous journals and anthologies, including *What Wildness Is This: Women Write about the Southwest; Global Warming: Collection of Poems; So West: Love Kills;* and *What We Talk about When We Talk about It: variations on the theme of love* I, II. Finishing Line Press recently released her chapbook of poems, *Making Silent Stones Sing*.